In Praise of Aunts

In Praise of Aunts

M.R.Peacocke

PETERLOO POETS

First published in 2008
by Peterloo Poets
The Old Chapel, Sand Lane, Calstock,
Cornwall PL18 9QX, U.K.

© 2008 by M.R.Peacocke

The moral rights of the author are asserted in accordance
with the Copyright, Designs and Patent Act, 1988

All rights reserved. No part of this publication may be
reproduced, stored in a retrieval system, or transmitted,
in any form or by any means, electronic, mechanical,
photocopying, recording or otherwise without the prior
permission in writing of the publisher.

**A catalogue record for this book is available
from the British Library**

ISBN 9781904324492

Printed in Great Britain
By 4word Ltd, Unit15, Baker's Park, Bristol BS13 7TT

ACKNOWLEDGEMENTS

Some of these poems have appeared in *The Edinburgh Review, Granta, The New Humanist, The North*. "By the Canal" was included in the second series of *Oxford Poetry Broadsides, 2006* in a limited edition numbered 1 – 75. "In Praise of Aunts" was commended in the *Troubadour* competition, 2007.

Supported by
The National Lottery®
through Arts Council England

ARTS COUNCIL ENGLAND

For Tamsin, Tully, Barnaby and Hattie.

CONTENTS

11	In Praise of Aunts
12	The World and Mrs Elphinstone
13	Refuge
14	Ozymandias Resurgens
15	Jato
16	Fear No More
17	By the Canal
18	A Name
19	Kestrel
20	The Blind Men Look at an Elephant
21	Red
22	The Traveller on the Road
23	Fair
24	When a Butterfly Flaps its Wings
25	Winter Solstice
26	Witness
27	Wheatfield under Thunderclouds
28	Gowbarrow Park
29	A Window in Tours
30	The Place
32	Waking
33	Simile
34	Checklist
35	"How nimble the old are"
36	Running
37	The Bus
38	Sunday Diary
39	Hulk
40	Dreaming of Trains
41	Her Photo
42	The Nothing
43	Wordnurse
44	Wrong Door
46	No One
47	Potatoes

48	Afternoon
49	Reader
50	The Look
51	The Value of X
52	Still Life
53	An Evening in New Jersey
54	The Eyes in the Street
55	Mother Moon
56	Stoat
57	Dog
58	Cookie
59	Meadow
60	Milking Time
61	Spider
62	Gardener
63	Taurus
64	The Hunt

In Praise of Aunts

I conjure Aunts, sly laughers,
Aunts not of the blood
but of the spirit; invite
from their cold cots for scones and tea
Aunts who could cheat
and fib for fun, playing Old Maid
in silent riot, keeping a card
up a knickerleg; Aunts who would never
hurt a child to do it good;

Aunts without men, good sports,
bachelor Aunts eternally retired
who liked dogs, who could whistle,
Aunts with pockets, pocketsful
of small timely treats,
and not wincing at stickiness
nor at blood as they strode
through the war, through the wards,
voluntary servant goddesses.

You women long at peace,
rooted in sycamore scrub
beneath St. Peter's topsyturvy stones
without memorial: I will praise
your names, your dented hats and bulging shoes,
who pedalled across my dream
last night with shining spokes and hubs
and cracked halloos and glimpse of knees,
old children in your upright childless bones.

The World and Mrs Elphinstone

The weekly shop, time for a cup of tea before the bus,
the basket snug against her lisle calves and her thick brown purse
on the cloth, pennies, shillings, her ticket home, ration books
(clipped), the butcher in a good mood today, a bit extra,
enough coupons left for   Except that   Only a small bomb,
close to the Green, the cinema showing *Hellzapoppin* –

Brown coat ripped wide, decent corset, kidneys and breast of lamb.

Suppose after the engine coughed, someone had shouted up
to the young reconnaissance pilot checking his gear, Oh –
(the prop is spinning to a blur) good luck, and by the way,
on your route home when the coast's in sight, while you're about it
just kill Mrs Elphinstone, would you? Wearing a felt hat.
Fifties, about your mother's build: might the world be different?

Refuge

It was after a war, one of the wars.
It was under a bridge, one of the bridges,
where a swollen river jostled for the sea.

What can be said of the stone eyelid
of a bridge? In that canthus a head may shelter,
propped shadowy head in which the eyes are wounds.

It was back in the stench and shadow of the bridge
that a head lay and turned its wounds on me.
The wounds were mouths whose tongues had been excised.

Affliction bears no name or passport;
crosses what must be crossed. It is a slow yeast
that raises after years, enough years, a sour loaf.

Affliction casts its bread on the water;
crouches to lap at the swollen water; does not
pity itself; sleeps where it falls, or dies.

Affliction is the leper bidden to cry
Unclean, Unclean, and may happen on refuge
as grit embeds at random in an eye.

Ozymandias Resurgens

I met a traveller from an antique land
Who showed me film of Ozymandias ruin'd
And said, Time is an axe: this ancient sprawl
Of stone half-buried shows how tyrants fall.
That threatening brow and outstretched arm
Have lost all power to harm,
Monument only of some crude romance.
A harsh wind blew. I saw the dry sand dance,
And, as I watched, the stones began to stir,
And join, and rise. A cracked Kapellmeister
Loomed on his dais, grotesquely uniformed;
On grasping fists a thousand searchlights beamed.
Yelling in admiration or dismay,
A jostling horde of slaves stretched far away.

Jato

Jato is dead, so he won't be scrambling
to an internet café to tell me
for himself. When I try the frequencies,
what comes through is just the Guernica scream
you can't switch off; but I think he's laughing
about the mosquitoes of Maroua
still trying to suck out his shadow blood
till he's slapped himself rigid. Since the world's
turveyed to a negative, it's child's play
to handle a Kalashnikov; and when
the midday sun comes hammering at doors,
who can you trust to say what's light, what's dark?

Jato Nyanganji, journalist and poet.

Fear No More

No longer afraid of the sun's fury
the bayonets of winter or the zealotry
of the fly who has soldiered in his green cuirass
through the torn centuries as far as this

No longer wretched under the gun's rage
but taking leave to attend the marriage
of dust with dust or surrendered
to the physic of grass   nettle   root   reed

And now their consummation
respectful exhumation
Silent histories taken
from a rag or a button

Each mad impromptu grin
seemly under supervision
A name ascribed   A stone
to note the task as done

But who can yet be sure
that every ghost is laid
and the wages of fear
finally and fully paid?

By the Canal

To have tumbled crud over wheels
one distant afternoon: and did it fall
or was it a trudge
to subterranea where the long boats chug,

and push coming to shove – the labour! –
that final heave over railing or brick:
an olive splash
in the oily canal, chrome ribs airward

that had transported packet delights,
sullen potatoes, nets of oranges
(two for the price of,
before the greyblue mould began to bloom),

tubs of fats, chicken legs, burgers,
lilies two-ninety-nine? The daily round
the common task
should furnish, etcetera, but won't erase

a taste for the cinder road,
the narrowing ruts, the towpath track.
Derry down derelict the world veers round,
faltering; dumped.

A Name

(Spenser: *Amoretti* LXXV)

One day I wrote her name upon the strand,
      picked up some black briny stick, scratched it
      deep into translucent grit;
But came the waves and washéd it away.
Agayne I wrote it with a second hand,
But came the tyde, the slather and lick, feet
      sidelined and sliding, all the letters drowned.
For I myselve shall lyke to this decay.
      Platitudes of renewal, cure
      or comfort drag me down.
      How we were, what we are is washed away,
      the tidal whisper, escher, escher, escher,
      fish become bird, wing become fin,
      no joy. Let it be done.

Kestrel

Kestrel, small masterful falcon: I'd have you
nothing beyond yourself. Let me not see you
as symbol; no minion; your shudder
on the tilting air never the posture
of a servant before his lord.

That outsling from the clough, traverse, brilliant
plunge and rise from the soaked grass
with laden talons, hunger taught
at the rim of a charnel nest.
Wild blood's the apple of your perfect eye.

The Blind Men Look at an Elephant

So this one extends his diffident fingers
to a leg. Towering warm! Scarred with crisscross
indentations like the bark of the tree
he'd climb when he was young, toes gripping, arms tossed
another rung higher to his airy hide.
A tree, a tree, this elephant, his haven!
while the next catches hold of the tail. What's this?
Hair, coarse and soft – and he's crying, remembering
his grandmother at the wash tub, her grey locks
escaping and dapping the suds, the one soul
who loved him and his foolish eyes.
                                          One man leans
his head against the rumbling belly: uncles!
All five of them snoring in the midday sun.
His brother's caught hold of an ear. He's stroking
the leathery thinness and his hand recalls
those lily leaves, lotus, how pliable they were
and cool in the temple gardens where he'd pray.
Last, the weight of the trunk: how a great serpent
lay across a boy's thin shoulders like hard silk
while a pipe screamed in his ears and screamed and screamed –
and everyone's laughing at these simpletons
in the zoo park, their white eyes and how they grin;
but they're wrapped in the dream of their knowledge, safe,
their shadowy hearts blessed in the haygreen smell
of an elephant, its patience and its peace.

Red

What's inside the shell?
Inside the shell there's a shell
and inside that another and inside that
another one smaller; but when you reach
the very last one, wait! A red dot
like a blood prick on your finger.

She's bowing over the stove,
a tiny scarfed Baboushka, stirring
the soup with a Russian spoon.
She's shaking the goosefeather bed.
She's singing in a splintery
minuscule voice. Are you going to knock?

Remember she didn't invite you.
What will you say when she looks up
with her cranberry cheeks, her eyes
black as full stops, and skips nearer,
and gets bigger, and unlocks
her nipping wooden teeth?

The Traveller on the Road

Where are you going?
To Troy, my dear, Jerusalem
or Babylon, depending.
The Moon if there's a boat.

How do you travel?
Lightfooted lightheaded lighthanded.
What will you find?
Hungers. Pop 'em in a sack.

Who keeps you company?
My bones my bones
and my little small dog
who's a jacksmith.

Meet anyone? Aye.
All the spring shouters
the lickety queens
and the rogues of the field.

May I come with you?
He will twitch her away
and there she'll dance
in the quick of his eye.

Fair

So they hobble away on bleeding feet.
Shadowy corridor, green baize, grand stair.
One is clutching the arm of the other
above the elbow. *Well don't hold so tight,
you pinch! Anyway, all she did was sit
in the hearth, built herself a better fire
than we ever had! Lolled in the corner,
the slut! What did she do to deserve it?
We suffered enough to be beautiful,
didn't we? At least, I did. You should've –*
Dust greys the backs of every velvet chair.
*Don't be in such a hurry! Oh, don't pull!
I'm the eldest, I should have got the love!*
Echoes are bickering: *Not fair – fair - fair ...*

When a Butterfly Flaps its Wings

If you should sneeze, imagine: southeast of here
    the forests may begin to stir –
    Bohemia, Carpathia – and European bison
lift their muzzles, dreaming and stamping after green,

while further on, the mighty thornback fishes of the Black Sea
    which squinted once at Argo's keel
    may be shaken at the depth like carpets
dragged to the spring air from Mongolian yurts

and all this widening turbulence ride on,
    spreading like a delta – Sakhalin, Canton –
    flattening bamboo groves and gingko trees,
the tiny confusion of your single sneeze

startling the immense Pacific; but, what about
the rest, the westward hurtling sneezes: won't they
        cancel yours out?

Winter Solstice

I'm reading an old wives' tale –
about swallows: how, come winter,
so the belief was, they'd hibernate
deep in the mud of ponds, transmogrified
to frogs: frogrified.

Half past six, my clock says; then
it's been saying the same for months,
but we don't quarrel: clock sits there, I'm
over here, while the sun is managing
a slant manoeuvre,

peering in. Are you wanting
a story or the time, old sun?
Well, here are both: we're at the bottom
of the winter pond like frogs, gluey cold,
not saying a thing,

one hour stuck as another.
And yet something's about to turn,
to wake, blink, shift, shine; and in no time
there'll be a skyful of swallows racing
back and full of talk.

To witness miracles you don't need
to be chosen   remarkable   possessed of gifts
not even lucky over time and place   just
to be alive to what's there fizzing
like fish in a coral garden
brilliant exchanges among souls and worlds

Rub habit from your eye   you'll catch
astonishments such as rascally Jacob dreamed
angelic fooling   starry tricks
on a builder's ladder propped against heaven

Wheatfield under Thunderclouds

Auvers-sur-Oise, July 1890 (Vincent van Gogh's last painting)

Courage   Patience   It's going to rain
What if these tangs of carmine
poppybloodclots   had not
roped me stupid as a colt
into the foreground clay   the
stubble is it   had not dragged
my boots towards that lake of green
where all's intent on drowning

then what could have stopped me
stumbling off the horizon
where dark blue thunder's massing
against Auvers   *De scheppingskracht
kan men niet*   can't hold it back
the power mumbling and building
over the wheat towards Auvers
and the gut cries of clouds

De weğ om te slağen is
The way to succeed is
(*Courage   Patience*) to decide
between green and blue

(Quotations are from Vincent's letters to his brother Theo)

Gowbarrow Park

(Dorothy Wordsworth's Journal, April 15th 1802)

Cut home by the woodpath, nearer the lake.
More shelter perhaps among the hazel.
The bitter wind tugs at her skirt and shawl.
Bony umbrella, old blue cloak,
He's striding ahead, loud boots on the gravelly track,
His shoulders hunched against the whip of twigs,
Mumbling to himself. ('Bum, bum, bum, old numbly legs'
The village lads call slily.) If he looked back
He'd glimpse the first of the April dancers –
Daffodils, singly and scattered – a crowd – thousands –
Pale as new butter against the sear and gleam
Of the lake; and motionless
Among them, braced in the wind,
Absorbed, her slight frame.

The stragglers, the little knots –
"Nothing to disturb the simplicity,
Unity and life of that one busy highway."
Despite harsh weather, nothing to spoil delight.
Long after that day's furious wind and wet
He'll sift her Journal: what he'll choose
Are resonant words not hers:
'Golden', and 'jocund'; 'sprightly'; 'poet':
Pleased with the unity of those,
Invent a sparkling day,
A pensive self, a blissful solitude.
Her truth keeps room for dance and brokenness,
Hunger with joy: what holds her inward eye,
Deer like skeletons in the leafless wood.

A Window in Tours

A taxidermist's window,
in Tours: a tremendous poodle,
rigged to perfection, buttoned
with glassy discs, every hair in place.

Madame, whose platonic passion
bought for this coiffed gentilhomme
a limited immortality:
in case you too were gazing

that day in daguerrotype
from some parlour wall, and the sun
happened to slant across your blanched cheek,
I've wanted to tell you this:

a mouse – don't flinch – came toddling
modest as a chantry priest
on a visit to your darling,
processed – I saw it that afternoon –

among the four pillar legs,
inspected an onyx nail, and,
just as a dusty sunbeam struck, danced
like David before his Lord;

so, while you may not have been blessed
by the chaste saint you prayed to
and no one, rose in hand, knocked,
there's still a witness to your parched love.

The Place

After the rain, I found a broadcloth valley
steaming where it was spread,
weighted at the hem with woods.
Somewhere a thrush called *deo, deo*.

I walked in the drenched silence,
followed upstream through tumbling grasses
a muffled watervoice
headlong with sibilants;

and soon not one stream
but many, ran in the meadow
like ducklings, a little, low
bridgestone here and there to cross them –

yet maps won't show me the place -
or any pamphlet or green guide –
or tell me where I was heading, or how I made,
that morning, my pilgrimage of grace.

Where can it be, that crumbling chapel
the water led me to,
with pencilled messages, *Deo,
Deo Gratias*, stubbed into the limewashed wall:

Thanks to our Lady, our blessed Lord,
for a safe birth, a haemorrhage staunched, release from pain,
Marie almost recovered; for Jean, Claude, Célestine;
for Mother's health miraculously restored.

Where is the plaster Virgin, bleached hood
and downcast smile, the few scattered coins,
the woollen shoe, the silver pins,
the unrolled bandage rusty with blood?

I was there, there once, there somewhere
in a broad unpeopled valley –
Brittany was it or Low Normandy? –
without desire except to chance my pleasure;

and found God's hut,
built to trap mercies or as a store
for blessing, where the untrammelled water
sprang into fleeting light.

Waking

Light rakes through all the wincing cavities of the skull,
marshalling, sieving through angles and slouch; filters up
recollection of a long hinged placing and steadying,
stern and stem, shipbone rouse and settle; until it wakes,
reluctant body; hauls up its ragged shadow, leans
to the day, secures a self; resumes its lively scars.

Simile

Like waking on a clear day early, satisfied with sleep,
and stretching, when the stretch takes you and widens you
                                                   further
than the narrow arches of the body knew they could go,
widens you and flings you softly to your furthest of touch –

this simile that I know and don't know, that won't attach,
that's like the moth I found on the floor, white, plumy, perfect
except that something had gone out of it; or else perhaps
a flawless immobility had crept in; and this moth

resembles the dream whose loss I wake to, that's telling me
the vital thing I need to know which waking displaces,
like the smell of a loved body that once seemed like the smell
of love itself and now you can't, can't recall. Can't recall.

Checklist

Have you a name or distinguishing feature?
Do you suffer from any sensory deception?
Are your eyes male or female?

Have you passed any port/strait gate /needle's eye?
Would you describe yourself as insurgent resurgent
deciduous or snowy?

Is this your body? Did you pack it yourself?
Are you to your best knowledge and belief?
Append proof.

"How nimble the old are"

How nimble the old are, balancing
as the world gyrates beneath them   fast   faster
All that's familiar sweeps from touch
till their bones are honeycomb

You can't know how deftly I'm spinning
or how I love anything that hesitates
pauses sticks with me a minute
touches my flying head   Look

I've gathered a little parchment leaf
It settled against my cheek as damp and cool
as a child's kiss   We have happened
together   We slip away

Running

Once there was running, a spurt of joy
in the feet, unbidden, some riot
under the skin.
Later there was running, willed.
Now the body's dull
like the lips of grazing animals
mumbling at frozen glass. If I say,
Do you remember running?
It pauses, puzzled. It has its tasks.
It can't recall.

The Bus

A stiff climb, the three steps. He opens a brown fist
and counts out the right fare. Five rows back most often,
the shady side today. Shady side today, aye. A' right, Ted?
A' right, aye. Tweed sleeve sits by tweed sleeve most Saturdays;
today one lean brown arm settles alongside another.

The bus eases away, chirruping and groaning, heaving
at bends. The lane turns: below them a chequered valley
shines, familiar as a kitchen, and there is nothing
to be said of it, they know it like a mother. Their talk
is all of vegetables, the trenching and ridging,

hoeing and forking. Purple-top it's too warm, split at the core.
Peas gone dry and the spinach bolting. Taties I don't
know. Corn, though, corn and tomatoes. Marrows, aye.
Come October give the Lord his due with a good mixed basket
at the altar steps and a monstrous blue cabbage.

Special prize at the Show that ought to get. Aye.

Eloquence is fading now. A few more weeks until the time
of caps, oiling of tools, storing away, and winter to be endured
like a sleepless night. Past the big estate, roundabout,
Ford garage. Hospital the next stop. Now then, Ted.

Sunday Diary

Vicar came, soft hands and smiling.
A little talk with God amen
and later there was Songs of Praise.

Lovehate the rightness righteousness
of hymn tunes, how the harmonies
move in step like nuns, supportive
maintenance of the melody
(like women's underwear, modest
but assured and feeling we hope
nice.) The holy paths of the tunes
are for those among us younger
or unsure of holding a part.
Sometimes there's the very top-floor
extravagance of a descant
above the secure foundations
but then in due course down we go
safe and sound, cadence descending
with the no-nonsense of a lift
achieving ground level. How sweet
the thought of Sunday closing, bells,
churchwardens, choirboys and good news
of a wedding with proper banns –
and yet my spirit won't be still,
keeps up its butterfly shuffle
unreconciled against the pane,
its dusty lisp, craving the light,
the wild cold air that will kill it.

Hulk

Rusting encumbered hulk, you may sink
when you like, zigzag darkwards,
founder. I want to be shot of you.
With one deft shudder if I could
I'd grow permeable, translucent,
flex through barnacled plates and strakes,
skinny-dip upwards, flow
into enormous light, breathe light,
shimmer and refract – but the cramped
submariner heart that's spent so long
labouring below decks is deaf
with habit, turns its back on me, tinkers
among its dirty oils and won't give in.

Dreaming of Trains

Dreaming of trains. What did they do before trains, I mean for
                                            dreams?
You take your bags and you step down, clunk the door goes
                                          double clunk,
green flag, whistle and off she goes, shrinking to vanishing point
and there you are, dumped, no cabs, it's like destiny's not
                                              working.

That time though, that was real. Honiton Junction, stiff in
                                            civvies
and the girl at the window riding away, her black soft hair.
She wouldn't give me her address. Well when you're young
                                            I suppose
you're in love with love. She must've had a lad down in
                                            Plymouth.

Some's like the birds in winter, come for what they need, then
                                            gone.
The two lines, far enough off you'd think they kissed but they
                                            don't.

Her Photo

I filch memories from other heads.
For example this photo (source unknown) taken
when summer was dense among the leaves:
not waking not sleeping, the fine hair flowing back.

The colour of the day still sparkles
in her absence on the tip of my tongue; the words
I can't hear, that were settling round her,
return at times like swallows with the songs and names.

The Nothing

The man of pain cries "Bless
your servant with your emptiness."
Emptiness. He palps it like the gap
where teeth were once, to try its shape.
Where's an edge? Where is the living hurt?
What isn't there's inert,
Elusive; tempts a probing tongue
to query and beg and bargain:
"Immortal god of everything and nothing,
rather than nothing, give me pain."

Wordnurse

    She's popping in
wearing a word mask
      round eyes slit mouth

    trotting across
in patent word shoes
      neat word apron

    Time to set up
a word drip Tap tap
      look for a vein

    elbowing out
the blessed silence
      No words today

    thank you   but Oh
she cries We'll have you
      as right as rain

    I say No   please
don't change the dead bulbs
      I want my dark

    but she's smiling
clipping new fuses
      to my eyeballs

    plugging me in
jacking me alive
      Now then just a

    little wordsip
(let's make sure nothing
      is understood)

Wrong Door

Down too many corridors, a lift
glissading, ticking off Two One B
and out, to step by mistake into
a depository of mistakes,
some sort of Musee de l'Homme, museum
of human anomaly (the light
through the afternoon a clear fluid
yellowish beyond the heavy glass,
the to and fro of traffic muffled)
and What's this? The rows of lucid jars
labelled and shelved, catacomb, larder.

Moving onwards like a châtelaine;
an appraisal of preserves. Here's
a slice, hard coral of lung, tarry
(*she* must have died like that), a potted
vermiform thing, arachnoid clusters
and I'm visualising the haslet
in Mr Gray's shop down Cleeve Street,
the faggots wrapped in muslins of caul.
Now, that's what started life as a big
toe, *Big Toe of Policeman*, formal
in formaldehyde (locked up here, boot's
on the other foot.)

              Hilarity
spurts out of shock, questionable jokes,
the brain alight with supposition,
simile, history, and pinched with fear.
How did I get into this pickle,
lone haruspex combing through the aisles?
In a side chapel my self is pulled

together, meeting the tiny priest
face to face, his closed lids, his helmet –
blanched enormous rasta-hat of bone:
pooka, bottled goblin, someone's child.

No One

A voice in the orchard
when I was digging. *Here I am,
hair and bone.
Don't hide me again!
One more waking, one more bite
of the apple, one more dance.
Don't cut me dead.*

A cloud put out the sun. My spade
struck on stone.
No one.

Potatoes

(Reminiscences of the old women of Longtown)

Morning till night   In the end
You couldn't straighten   you were that
    That stiff   The cold and the picking

Used to sing Rose did   Lovely
A good day they give us a whole
    Whole apronful of potatoes

Clogs they wore then   And our mothers
They wouldn't now   Wear a man's cap
    They used to   Everybody did

And in the evening sit outside
Smoke a clay pipe   They give us
    a whole   Yes   That Rose   Lovely

Afternoon

The wool rolls down. The needles droop.
A spider at the corner pane
Schemes for a pittance line by line.
The dull doves in the neighbouring wood
Call Could you do   Do do   You could.
A wakeless lull that's less than sleep
Brims in her eyes and palms and lap.
Something is finished. Nothing's done.
A lapse, a loss, a truce, a peace.
One lacewing trembles at the netted glass.

Reader

Did I tell you about the journey?
We stopped beyond a station. Quite dark.
There might have been gardens.
There was a woman with her book.
She was looking up – look of absorption
some children carry or the newly dead –
she was peering in. Then the slide began
and she blew away. I haven't forgotten.
What was she reading out there?
She had something to tell, something
I needed to hear. Where the lines meet
and in the broken hedges will be words
like castaways, odd shoes, a tattered wing.

The Look

Once, David Hockney looked at me.
I was wearing a long dress, red.
His look cut through the flourish of that
and through my skin – less diaphanous –
the reds beneath it – butcher colours –
down to the bone. It didn't hurt.
I'd been appraised and dissected
in no time, and he'd looked away.

Yolk-yellow hair, round glasses –
like a Warhol print – all I could register;
but I was struck, just then, with double vision:
ambling along, or angled in a chair,
for a while afterwards my skeleton
observed itself through curious socket eyes.

The Value of X

Some nights I'm obliged to go down once more
by the light of my skin, fingers testing
diagonals and verticals, toes curled
over the treads, to seek out
the nub of the lamp and startle it
onto a gallery of objects

just to check on her: and yes, there she is,
unfinished as ever, blocked face sleepless hair
boxed in the cube of window glass;
and we stare at each other, two halves
of an equation, still at a loss
how to deduce the value of X.

Still Life

Silence of heads   Your head   my head
across from each other like books

I have known silences that howled
or where birds grew leaden and fell

Our silence rustles like a page
being turned   being read   unread

Lemons in a seablue bowl   Where
was colour before this present?

We are still lives   alive and still
We are light in a prism   at rest

An Evening in New Jersey

MeMeMe cicada cries, blunting
the edge of his multiple discourse
against the burned-out day, and steadies
an oak tree upright with his hooked feet,
his millions of self alone.
                                  Dusk.
In shadowy gardens, single frogs
are starting to chant, ManyMany,
ManyMany. A girl on the porch
deplores in a grieving monologue
the brevity of day-lily loves,
while stars ignore us, tapping their codes
among the blackmost boughs, and the moon
offers itself like an empty bowl.

The Eyes in the Street

A way of looking –
a bold-eyed brass-button look
a broadside lookahoy mockery
whatyerlookinat look

or a lookbehindyer
curtain-twitcher slippery
narrowing nothroughroad a
nimby not-looking look –

whether a roadlong sidling stare
or sidelong riddling leer streetwise
or in disguise the eyes
have it. You have to survive it.

Mother Moon

Day shuts, and the last rose blackens,
the red plucked from it. I am blind,
almost, till the full moon stares out.

You, according to your habit,
would note her smile, benevolent
she-moon. I'd keep it to myself,

the fossil skull I saw, its closed
amusement. (How is it that we can't
read anything but these seemings?)

Now you're absent I forget you,
like that same old flat-battery
vanished invisible sunk moon,

but you come again. You're in me,
part of me whether I like it
or not; and I soften, thinking

of churlish impromptu visits,
and the trug, and the secateurs,
and your deft heavy hands snipping

the choicest blooms, and lifting down
a silver bowl and arranging
roses for my very own room.

Stoat

Stoat nips by, not seen till he's gone – something
about a shadow, a tail hanging
by the topstone and flickering on – there
at the crevice, that's where he crosses
into my line of sight – that's where he lives,
somewhere in the drystone wall; quests out –
intimation of him – about his meal
when I'm near the window getting mine –
is he aware of my look behind glass?

Turn on the radio, wonder about lives
in the built environment, holed up,
wary, the fangs and eyes – oh yes, I see
I've been angry today – recognise
the quick hidden beast desirous of blood
(and how well schooled it seems I must be,
brightly concealing my unruly selves
most of the time from my ruly self.
That kind of education: it's costly.)

Dog

Dog goes skeltering by
and snouts, at any tuft
or corner, hero dog
heroine dog or enemy
in pungent scrit.

Fine tail taut shoulder
circle his feelings out
in riffs of playing war
or the waging of love,
a mesh of self and other.

All that he is of joy
boredom attention dream,
need and desire the same,
speaks in pulls of muscle
under a lithe skin,

but voice and naked hand
have claimed him nerve and heart
and have his measure.
Dog is bound, endures
awake, asleep, leashed by his name.

Cookie

A woollen kind of dog,
patient, who knows engines, though the right one
has still to sound.
She sits on the doorstep,
waiting. She looks for the resurrection
of the dead – not
all of them, just the one
who'll be holding a heavenly biscuit,
expecting her.

Meadow

      Steady swaddle and rip
of the heifers' tongues altering
      surfaces   Sweep and crop
of grass becoming flesh   The gleam
      slips from flowerhead to hide

      This one lifts her muzzle
from the slow devouring   gives me
      a cloudy stare and wades
further into the afternoon
      with a soft smash of stems

Milking Time

An old cow swaying homeward crushes
the exhausted grass of October
pace by pace. The sap of one more day
has drained her heavy udder.

She finds her place. Electric bulbs mark
her blacks and whites, mechanical throats
strip her and lighten her, a pale juice
seethes, becoming measurable.

She feeds. Melancholy pools her eye.
She has grieved for each of the eight calves
that have nuzzled her leathery flanks
as each has been taken away.

Spider

This is her world: potting shed window
that the sun today smears through, warming
her heatless body at the sheer gleam.

Spider: headhelmet studded with eyes,
thread waist, abdomen speckled and humped,
eight striped legs minutely hooked, expert.

Blunder into her geometries
and she leaps out, palping and testing
and repairing every broken guy.

Her stillness is urgent, her tensions
a netted stillness. My breath on her:
what does she feel? Does she hear or smell?

What told her to prepare this grey nest
from which her children are trickling, bead
by pinpoint bead, each an amber life,

translucent, invisibly leggy,
abseiling down the wall of the air?
Does she love them? Know that they are hers?

What kind of knowledge sits in her shape?
Twang, she goes, and abruptly vibrates,
seizes on a trapped bug, to suck it.

Suppose her bigger: as big as me.
Her cable could wind me and wrap me
into a blindfold mummy, deaf, dry.

Gardener

Swifts are long gone, and swallows
absent now; only the dry leaves
chicker before a flight.

A level sun, gilding
the bushes and green corners,
settles – there – on your bending back

like a hoverfly, so light
you scarcely feel it, diligent
among the little days.

Taurus

A red bull crossing the pasture
on splayed hooves, ponderous,
the clay stamped and sealed
beneath his bulk; his pulse, I thought,
the thud, thud of a maul.

How the dusk enlightens an eye.
The bull became swarthy
as a clot of blood,
his double plume of breath whitening
to an October frost.

Darkness at last grows luminous.
The stars I've learned are few,
but I should know you,
Taurus, your shape, at the high gate
of winter and alone.

The Hunt

Sunburnt hunting child
wading barelegged through the dry August rough
intent on catching lizards.

Black jumping spider –
that isn't it – scuffling mouse – grasshopper
flicketing out; as for luck –

what if luck were fanged?
Risk, though, sharpens a body to commit
to the pounce. Sometimes nothing.

Sometimes a frantic
whipping between hot palms. Open them slow,
slow as a scallop: peer in:

there may be a glint –
a defiant eye – and smooth panting flanks
and hooked toes ready to leap:

the triumph of it!
but what if it's a tail trunked off, bloodless
and still thrashing?
                    Tails you lose

like the words you believe
to be pulsing live – but they die on you,
the quick heart out of your grasp.